Journaling Advent

Your Journey Through Celtic Advent.

Passages, Poems, Prayers

Compiled by

Claire Burgess

A message from Chris McQuillen – Wright

The advent pilgrimage is one where we already know the end, the coming of the light of Christ to banish all darkness from our lives. It is though, a theological pilgrimage, time of preparation for an end already known. Our theology, our faith, our spiritual pilgrimage should reflect our true lives; lives where the ending is obscure, where we don't know what the next moment will hold.

Life changes in an instant and in our case, our daughter Rosey, her life changing event has altered the lives of all those around her. Jesus talks of being prepared for life changing moments and this is our advent pilgrimage. Not towards the certain knowledge pf Christmas but towards life defining moments that we cannot today possibly comprehend. Life is unknown except for the moment we live in, so slow these moments down, appreciate what is for the day that is now is all that we have.

Don't lose today in preparing for tomorrow for the Advent of our lives is already upon us. With much gratitude to Claire and her team of writers for penning these thoughtful, inspirational, and heartfelt reflections in aid of Rosey's rehabilitation Appeal, I commend this Advent Journey to you.

Chris

Breathe deeply and fill your body with life giving air
If you can, do it outside. Allow your eyes, ears, and nose to soak up nature.
Take in the wonder of creation. We are truly blessed.

With each new day you have the opportunity to refresh your journey.

The journey with yourself, your journey with your family and friends, your journey with strangers and your journey with God

Take a moment to reflect where you are on those journeys... You are not in a race, with yourself or with others.

God wants you to invite him along on your travels and through the trials and tribulations of life

God calls you to a life filled with love, forgiveness, and deliverance.

He hears the voice crying in the wilderness

He encourages you to bring Jesus into your heart so that his peace and love flow through you and beyond.

Advent and Christmas can be times of challenge.

Be patient, like the farmer waiting for the Autumn and Spring rains. They cannot control the weather any more than you can control what's out of your hands.

Allow yourself to feel contentment if not joy at this time. For what has been, is left behind.

Today, with Jesus' help, a heart filled with love can achieve wonderful things.

God will hold your hand if you let Him.

Sarah Jane Jasper

With grateful thanks to all who responded to my Facebook call for help and contributed their poetic responses to the readings throughout this book.

Sarah Jane Jasper – Introductory Poem

Kirsty Jack, Mary Judkins, Alison Shaw, Annie Henry,
Sophie Troczynska, Jill Adams, Lilac Johnston, Jane Horton,
Maggie Willmott, Derath Durkin, Beth Benham,
Ben Morgan-Lundie, Pam Nicolls, Lindsey Morgan-Lundie,
Philip Mountstephen, Gillian Barritt, Debbie McGregor,
Becca Bell, Caroline Shepherd, Claire Jones, Gret Woodason,
Jacqui Griffiths, Hugh Nelson, David Remick, Brian Davis,
The Penlee Cluster, Ellouise Allard, Grace Kanungha, Karen Austin,
Jenny Lockwood, Robin Thwaites, Sian Yates, Simon Cade, Joanna Swan, Maggie Dolbear, Margaret Miles, Kay Short, Claire Burgess, Martyn Pinnock.

Funds raised by this book will be donated to Rosey's rehab appeal. Find out more here https://gofund.me/ef2b8d75

Introduction

As you journey through the Celtic Advent period spend some time in quiet reflection and preparation.

The approach we are going to use is called Lectio Divina.
Lectio Divina is an ancient spiritual practice and is widely used by those living in monastic communities or those following a monastic rule or lifestyle.

Through Lectio Divina, we seek to experience the presence of God by reading, listening, praying, meditating, and contemplating.

Use each chapter of this book as a separate study.
There are blank pages for your own notes, thoughts, reflections, and prayers alongside the poems written by the Christians who responded to the texts along the way.

There is a whole page in each chapter for you to add the names of people that you want to pray for during advent. You can add prayers for your community and for the world.

Before you start, make sure you are comfortable, have a glass of water at hand.
Adopt the posture that helps you best experience and receive the presence of God.

When you are ready, read the chosen passage slowly, paying attention to each word, noting down the words and phrases which particularly attract your attention.

There is space in this book for you to journal as you go.
There may be words that resonate with you, words that puzzle you or phrases and concepts that you hadn't considered before.
If you like you can choose more than one version of the text. Maybe use the bible you are most familiar with alongside a different version.

Do the same words or phrases speak to you when you read from another version of scripture?
Do these variations of words change the emphasis of the text and your understanding of it?
Now that you have read, begin to meditate on the words or phrases that held your attention.
It may be helpful to repeat the word or phrase several times quietly to yourself.

What thoughts come to mind as you meditate?
Do aspects resonate with your own experience?
How do you the words or phrase you are meditating on make you feel?
Is God calling you to respond to the word or phrase?

If you are studying in a group, you could ask different people to read from the different texts and discuss the words and phrases that caught your attention.

If you are studying alone then you may like to use an audio version alongside your own bible.

After meditating on the text, set aside some time for prayer.
This can be as simple as telling God the words that he has spoken to you through the text and asking him to use it to bless and transform you. Be guided by your own thoughts and ask God to show you how to use his word to shape your heart so that it reflects his.
Spend time in gentle contemplation, focusing on God's presence.
You may feel the need to continue praying, or read the text again, or to write down any thoughts, phrases, insights, prayers.
You may wish to express yourself creatively by writing poetry, prayers, drawing or painting.

Advent One
15th November

Read or listen to Luke 3: 3 - 6
Meditate on the text, dwelling on the words or phrases that stand out to you.

Pray, talk to God about those things that he has brought to you in these verses or use the prayer below if you wish.

Contemplate the text, you may wish to use the suggested consider points to get you started.

Record your exploration of this text using words, prayer, poems, and images.

Prayer.

Everlasting God
As I prepare myself to begin this journey into Advent, I renew my commitment to following in your way.
Help me, to find stillness in the business of this season, to find time to reflect and time to give thanks.
Draw all who follow you together at this time of expectation, that all may experience your presence and hear your voice.
Help me to sing your song and be opened to following you in new ways.
Amen.

Consider.

During Advent we experience the joy of waiting. Most of us will be busy planning ahead and looking toward the coming of Christ.

What expectations or hopes do you have as you journey towards Christmas?

All our journeys are unknown,
filled with twists and turns,
highs and lows,

Our God loves all his children,
He knows our hearts, thoughts, and flaws
He wants us to choose him,

Which ever path we take,
we all make mistakes and sin,
with regrets that weigh us down,

To lighten our load,
forgiveness is key,
Forgiving ourself or others is not easy,

The purpose of our lives,
only God knows,
to end the hurt, forgive yourself and others,

We all need forgiveness,
the full outcome unseen,
Only God knows,
if we forgive we can be with him.

Helen Kirsten Jack / 'Kirsty', New Zealand

My Prayers – 15th November

NOTES

NOTES

NOTES

Advent Two
16th November

Read or listen to Colossians 3: 15 – 16a
Meditate on the text, dwelling on the words or phrases that stand out to you.

Pray, talk to God about those things that he has brought to you in these verses or use the prayer below if you wish.

Contemplate the text, you may wish to use the suggested consider points to get you started.

Record your exploration of this text using words, prayer, poems, and images.

Prayer.

God of callings
Thank you for calling me to be part of your Church.
I ask for you to take from me the burdens of stress and worry and to help me remain calm in the busy days ahead.
Your peace guards and rules my heart. Help me to stay patient and seek your will.
Help me to stay alert to the needs of those I encounter, that through my words and actions I spread the joy that can only be found in knowing your love and peace.
Amen

Consider.

Do you have a great desire to do something particular for God?
What is stopping you? What preparations are you making?
Are you praying that God shows you his divine plan? Or are you racing ahead, hoping that God will bless your plan?

"Be thankful."
An attitude of gratitude?
We say it often, but what does it mean?
"And be thankful" - really?
"Sing with gratitude in your hearts" - honestly?

'Thank you for the world so sweet. Thank you for the food we eat. Thank you for the birds that sing. Thank you God for everything.'

'Simples!' If only...

It's Advent. Busy. Christmas not far away. Help!!!! Where's our attitude of gratitude now?
Where is our thankfulness?

And what else? oh yes, peace.....
"Peace on earth, goodwill to all men."
Not in my house! Yet!
The Christmas checklist:
Planning? Worrying? Shopping? Cooking? Who's coming to stay?

NO! Not that sort of peace!
The peace Christ offers.
The 'peace of Christ' to rule in our hearts. "Easier said than done" you sigh.

Trusting God and knowing He's there. Is that what gives us peace?

The 'peace of Christ' - no matter what's happening. Jesus, the Prince of Peace, offers His peace.
It's a gift, an early Christmas present maybe?

Accept it? Saying thank you?
Being grateful
An attitude of gratitude?
Moving from worry towards trust in God.
Time in God's Word, the 'message of Christ', strengthening faith.
An attitude of gratitude?

Oh yes.
No matter what life throws at us,
especially at Christmas,
our well of peace — God himself — never runs dry.

Thank you, God, for coming to earth as a baby, for dying for my sin, for rising again and for ascending to your rightful home in heaven.

Help my unbelief.

Mary Judkins

My Prayers – 16th November

NOTES

NOTES

Advent Three
17th November

Read or listen to Colossians 3: 17
Meditate on the text, dwelling on the words or phrases that stand out to you.

Pray, talk to God about those things that he has brought to you in these verses or use the prayer below if you wish.

Contemplate the text, you may wish to use the suggested consider points to get you started.

Record your exploration of this text using words, prayer, poems, and images.

Prayer.

Heavenly Father
I thank you for all that you have placed before me today.
Draw me ever closer to you through your most gracious love.
Let my focus be on you and help me to be aware of your presence in all that I think, say, and do.
Amen.

Consider.

How do you prepare for your day? Does it start with focussing on God through prayer?
Advent is often filled with 'to do' lists. It's easy in the hustle and bustle of the day to lose sight of God.
Try pausing in quiet prayer for a few minutes before a new activity or encounter.
Where is God on your list?

Hope for the future.
All encompassed by love, joy
And peace.
Jesus in all things, for ever.

Alison Shaw

My Prayers – 17th November

NOTES

NOTES

NOTES

Advent Four
18th November

Read or listen to John 1: 1 - 14
Meditate on the text, dwelling on the words or phrases that stand out to you.

Pray, talk to God about those things that he has brought to you in these verses or use the prayer below if you wish.

Contemplate the text, you may wish to use the suggested consider points to get you started.

Record your exploration of this text using words, prayer, poems, and images.

Prayer.

Eternal Creator. All glory, honour and praise belong to you.
Thank you that in Jesus I have become a new creation.
Thank you that the word became flesh and dwelt among us.
Make me ready to receive you each day as I journey through this Advent season.
Help me to shine your light in the darkness.
Amen

Consider.

The opening verses of Johns gospel use the phrase "In the beginning" – what is the significance of this? What comes to mind when you hear those words?

What do these verses tell us about the nature of Jesus?

How can you, like John, bear witness to the light?

The Threshold

In the beginning
Love
Word
God
Life
Light

A man … John … spread the news
"Light is coming … get ready!"
but people preferred
to stay in the dark
they chose not to
explore the Light
discover the Truth
feel the Love
(Except a few
who still spread the news today,
the Light is never
going to go away)

This Advent we journey into darkness
and the Light will be born once more
inviting us to enter into
Love
Word
God
Life
Eternal Light

Will you cross the threshold?

Annie Henry

My Prayers – 18th November

NOTES

NOTES

NOTES

Advent Five
19th November

Read or listen to Matthew 1: 1 - 17
Meditate on the text, dwelling on the words or phrases that stand out to you.

Pray, talk to God about those things that he has brought to you in these verses or use the prayer below if you wish.

Contemplate the text, you may wish to use the suggested consider points to get you started.

Record your exploration of this text using words, prayer, poems, and images.

Prayer.

Generous God
Thank you for all those faithful souls who have walked with me on my spiritual journey. Thank you for the testimonies of faith of those I don't know but that I have read or heard about because of their great example.
I ask that you give me courage and strength to follow in your way and in the ways of those who have gone before me in the places I now tread.
Amen

Consider.

Think about those who have influenced your faith journey. How have they inspired you?
How can you pass on the gospel message to future generations?
Who do you think may be thanking God for YOU in the future?

A promise passed down
A hope clung to through the generations

Through father and son,
Through mother and child,
Through family and tribe and nation.
Through story and rite,
Through wisdom and tradition,
Through worship and sacrifice and devotion.

Through shepherds and kings,
Through outcasts and outsiders,
Through judges and prophets and human begins.
Through love and anger,
Through longing and despair,
Through life and death and new beginnings.

Through exile and deportation,
Through doing wrong, and trying to do what's right,
Through loss and destruction and finding anew,
Through listening and waiting,
Through dream and vision,
Through lament and prayer and praise.

Through the unexpected.

A promise is passed on,
A hope renewed,
A hope to hold onto and passed on through the generations.

Rev. Sophie Troczynska

My Prayers – 19th November

NOTES

NOTES

NOTES

Advent Six
20th November

Read or listen to Luke 1: 26 - 38
Meditate on the text, dwelling on the words or phrases that stand out to you.

Pray, talk to God about those things that he has brought to you in these verses or use the prayer below if you wish.

Contemplate the text, you may wish to use the suggested consider points to get you started.

Record your exploration of this text using words, prayer, poems, and images.

Prayer.

Son of God
The most Holy of babies, dwelling in the womb of Mary, so courageous, willing host of God incarnate.
Help me to say yes to your will, even when I don't fully understand what you want me to do.
Take all fear from me and send your holy angels to protect me, and your Holy Spirit to guide me.
Amen

Consider.

The next 10 days are focussed on the first coming of Christ, the incarnation.
Take your eyes off the cross for a few moments and think about how God, the creator of all things, came to live amongst us, and moved in our world alongside us, as one of us.
How does that make you feel?
Would you have said "yes" to God if you were Mary?
What is God wanting you to say YES to?

The Sacrifice of Faith

I had a strange visitor today,
See my hands still tremble.
I was singing and praising God for you – Joseph
The millstone ground the corn.

Favoured he said, the Lord is with me.
Do not be afraid.
I will give birth to a son – a King!
The millstone ground the corn.

I am a virgin – Joseph
How can this be.
The power of the most high will shadow me.
The millstone ground the corn.

Elizabeth will have a child too
In her old age – Joseph.
All is possible with God – you know.
The millstone ground the corn

I told the visitor that's ok
I will love this child of God.
You know I love you – Joseph
I wept alone – forlorn.

Jill Adams

My Prayers – 20th November

NOTES

NOTES

NOTES

Advent Seven
21st November

Read or listen to Luke 1: 39 - 56
Meditate on the text, dwelling on the words or phrases that stand out to you.

Pray, talk to God about those things that he has brought to you in these verses or use the prayer below if you wish.

Contemplate the text, you may wish to use the suggested consider points to get you started.

Record your exploration of this text using words, prayer, poems, and images.

Prayer.

Creator God
Thank you for all those who have shared their poems in this book. We thank you for allowing each of us a glimpse of their walk with you. May they all continue to sing your song for the rest of their days.
Inspire my heart, O Lord.
Amen

Consider.

As you read the Magnificat, Mary's song, think about the times that you have experienced feelings of joy or situations that have made your heart sing. Maybe put those feelings down on paper in whichever form suits you.

Listen to your favourite song, hymn or worship music and dwell with God for a while.
How can you sing a new song for the lord in your daily life?

Canticle upon a Visitation

Bearing great news in her message of greeting,
Mary arrives at the home of her cousin Elisabeth,
who exclaims at their meeting,
That her own babe leapt within her womb
At these wondrous words!

Filled with the Spirit and with great joy,
Elisabeth praises Mary for her faith,
She marvels that the mother of her Lord
Has thus been blessed, and that she believes
That nothing is impossible with God.

Mary extols God
She declares His greatness
And her delight in Him
Her spirit rejoices, and with humility and reverence
She now undertakes her great calling

She knows that to those who fear the Lord
He will show great mercy
She affirms that He brings down the proud
And that He raises those who are brought low

Two women, Mary, and Elisabeth
Blessed with a message of hope and abundance
Sing praises!

At Advent, as we light our wreaths with candles
At a time of expectant waiting and preparation
For the Nativity of our Lord
We too now wait to welcome Him into our hearts

Gaudete!

Lilac I. Johnston

My Prayers – 21st November

NOTES

NOTES

NOTES

Advent Eight
22nd November

Read or listen to Matthew 1: 18 - 25
Meditate on the text, dwelling on the words or phrases that stand out to you.

Pray, talk to God about those things that he has brought to you in these verses or use the prayer below if you wish.

Contemplate the text, you may wish to use the suggested consider points to get you started.

Record your exploration of this text using words, prayer, poems, and images.

Prayer.

Awesome God
Thank you for your continued guidance and protection.
"Do not be afraid" you speak to me in so many ways. Help me to recognise the angels in my midst.
Prepare me, as you prepared Joseph and Mary, to not be afraid, so that I may hear your voice clearly as I walk this advent journey.
Amen

Consider.

Do you believe that you have had an angelic encounter, or mystical experience? Or maybe a dream in which God spoke to you. How did you react? Did you doubt? Were you frightened or reassured?
If you haven't had such an encounter, think about those we would consider "angels in our midst" How has your encounter with them shaped your faith or response to a situation?

Joseph of Nazareth
poetically pondering on Matthew 1.18-25

Who were you really,
Joseph of Nazareth?

Some traditions –
and artists – portray you as
middle-aged, even old.
A wizened widower,
cradle-snatcher – as if!
to Mary's teenaged virgin
in perpetua?

I imagine you as
a younger man. Honest,
hard-working, full of
hope, ideals, all the energy
and passions of youth, like
the cutely virile version of the
Beeb's *Nativity*?

But who were you really,
Joseph of Nazareth?

What do we know about you?

Galilean wood-worker,
son of Jacob – was he
also a carpenter? Of
David's royal house and city,
proud lineage traced back
to Abraham. And now
betrothed to Mary.

Did her parents think
you were good enough for her?
Was it an arranged marriage
or a love match?
Or maybe both. If God has a hand
in these things, he must've picked you
for that long line of begats.

To be fair though, if you
were descended from
royalty, it strikes me that
your family branch of rulers
had come down in the world
quite a bit. I mean,
kings to carpenters.

But

then Mary shares the good news.
And just for one
horrified, halting heartbeat,
family honour unfurled
comes completely crashing down,
along with your wooing,
wedding-waiting world.

No option, you thought, except
a quiet, 'quickie' divorce. You were
a decent kind of man. But then
the angel's visit in your dreams
turns the story upside down
and right side up again. Of course.
Carpenters to Kings.

October 2022 Jane Horton

My Prayers – 22nd November

NOTES

NOTES

Advent Nine
23rd November

Read or listen to Luke 2: 1 - 5
Meditate on the text, dwelling on the words or phrases that stand out to you.

Pray, talk to God about those things that he has brought to you in these verses or use the prayer below if you wish.

Contemplate the text, you may wish to use the suggested consider points to get you started.

Record your exploration of this text using words, prayer, poems, and images.

Prayer.

Lord of Journeys
Over rocky terrain you no doubt stumbled, so many journeys you took. To Bethlehem in the womb, and on donkey into Jerusalem.
Lord, I thank you that you lead me, a bright light in the darkness, as I navigate curved roads and rocky paths.
Be with me on all my journeys this advent time.
Amen

Consider.

Do you have to make any special journeys as we approach Christmas? To visit family and friends? To deliver presents, food parcels or cards? How do you prepare for these journeys? Some of these journeys may not be easy. Do you offer them to God?

A couple travelling, like so many others,
Yet on a journey so very different.
Mary and Joseph, obeying the rules of the powerful
Whilst bringing a child who will change everything,
Whose power has no comparison.

Mary, carrying
Joseph, protecting
Parents, loving

A couple travelling, like so many others,
Yet on a journey so very different.
Meekly fulfilling creation's story,
Joseph bearing the ancient lineage,
Mary bearing eternity.

Mary, carrying
Joseph, protecting
Parents, loving
World, waiting

Messiah, coming

Maggie Willmott

My Prayers – 23rd November

NOTES

NOTES

NOTES

Advent Ten
24th November

Read or listen to Luke 2: 6 - 7
Meditate on the text, dwelling on the words or phrases that stand out to you.

Pray, talk to God about those things that he has brought to you in these verses or use the prayer below if you wish.

Contemplate the text, you may wish to use the suggested consider points to get you started.

Record your exploration of this text using words, prayer, poems, and images.

Prayer.

Saviour of the world
You took on human form, through humble birth and with no fanfare.
Help me to do your work, drawing attention only to you.
Be with me at my weakest moments and at my greatest triumphs, that all I am, do and say is used for your glory. Grant me the bravery and tenacity of your earthly parents, Mary, and Joseph.
Amen

Consider.

The account of the birth of Christ is limited to a single verse. Why do you think this is?
Does it seem strange to you, that the incarnation is understated?

Think of the common phrase "Love came down at Christmas" What does this mean for you?

Well, there they were! Just the two them - in Bethlehem.
A strange place, all alone, and so far from home.
Can you imagine the scene? There with no hospital,
not even a home birth! A birth all alone.
But O what a birth! A birth that would change the world!

Wowzers!

Did Mary expect that her time would come now?
So far from home and no family to share her load?
How precious her first born, yet so lowly a start –.
Yet Jesus came for the rich and also the poor
The haves and the have nots, and those in between.

So Amazing!

Mary wrapped him in cloths, and placed him in a manger,
No clean hospital cot, nor a midwife in sight!
No disinfectant, no clean space, not even a pain killer!
But oh, so much love, for love was Himself!
Such love did He show us! Much did she show us!

Gobsmacking!

But how did she feel? With this role thrust upon her,
what was she thinking? For it was a role she wasn't seeking,
yet a role she accepted, as such was her faith in her God.
She was the mother of God, the mother of Jesus.
O what obedience was this! What trust was this!

So Incredible!

And what about Joseph? What was he thinking?
He too was obedient; he too was so trusting.
But did he believe her? Or was he suspicious?
Yet whatever he felt, he too went with God's plan,
a plan that was foretold, a plan that was explained.
Love came down at Christmas, and Oh so much love.

Trusting! *Revd. Derath Durkin*

My Prayers – 24th November

NOTES

NOTES

NOTES

Advent Eleven
25th November

Read or listen to Luke 2: 8 - 20
Meditate on the text, dwelling on the words or phrases that stand out to you.

Pray, talk to God about those things that he has brought to you in these verses or use the prayer below if you wish.

Contemplate the text, you may wish to use the suggested consider points to get you started.

Record your exploration of this text using words, prayer, poems, and images.

Prayer.

Lord Jesus, Great shepherd of the sheep,
Thank you for all those that have helped me see and follow you.
Thank you that you hear me when I cry out to you. Help me to trust you for you know what is best for me.
Help me to stay alert to your voice and to your call on my life.
Show me where you want me to go, guide me towards those who need you.
Amen

Consider.

Think about the first time you met Jesus. How did he find you? What did it take for you to follow him? Did others play a part in your faith story? How? Do you thank God for those people?

"Mummy, I'm going to be a shepherd at school "
my son said to me one day.
"I need a tea towel to put on my head
 and do you know anyone with a spare bale of hay?
We need it to put a dolly on
 it's supposed to be baby Jesus.
We have to go visit him,
after the angels came to see us.

my friend Lizzy is an angel,
she has bare feet!
Her auntie made her a dress,
out of an old white sheet
James is an angel,
and Alice is one too.
they come to visit all the shepherds
to tell us what to do.

James is the bossy one
and says, "a baby is born today,"
and that we must all go to Bethlehem
to see the dolly in the hay.
We practice every lunchtime.
We have to get it right.
Because the baby Jesus was born
on this special night.

And when you come to watch us
you and dad and uncle Todd,
we will tell you all the story
that led us to the Son of God.

Beth Benham

My Prayers – 25th November

NOTES

NOTES

NOTES

Advent Twelve
26th November

Read or listen to Luke 2: 21 - 38
Meditate on the text, dwelling on the words or phrases that stand out to you.

Pray, talk to God about those things that he has brought to you in these verses or use the prayer below if you wish.

Contemplate the text, you may wish to use the suggested consider points to get you started.

Record your exploration of this text using words, prayer, poems, and images.

Prayer.

Almighty Father,
Thank you that you have been with me since my birth, thank you for making me just as I am. Help me to know that I am 'enough' as I am. You have made me in your image, and I know that with you I am truly loved.
Be with me as each day unfolds, let me walk in your light and show me how to ease the darkness in the lives of those you place before me.
Amen

Consider.

Do you believe God has a plan for your life?
How do you discern which is the next step for you to take as daily life unfolds? How do you deal with the unexpected twists and turns life takes? Are you a reactor or a reflector?

Anna

When I look at you
what do I see?
The face of someone
who has been widowed
for longer
than most lifetimes.

A care-worn face
Gaunt from fasting
Pale from lack of sun
tired hands held
in ceaseless praise.

I noticed your reaction
to the voice of brother Simeon
declaring the fulness of his heart
to the Lord our God
and the child in his arms.

The quickness of your movement
to the side of his family
belied your years.
In your heart you knew
He was the One.

In that moment
as you praised and sang
that you were a child of God
a sister to the Child Jesus
complete and loved.

Ben Morgan-Lundie

My Prayers – 26th November

NOTES

NOTES

NOTES

Advent Thirteen
27ᵗʰ November

Read or listen to Matthew 2: 1 - 12
Meditate on the text, dwelling on the words or phrases that stand out to you.

Pray, talk to God about those things that he has brought to you in these verses or use the prayer below if you wish.

Contemplate the text, you may wish to use the suggested consider points to get you started.

Record your exploration of this text using words, prayer, poems, and images.

Prayer.

Lord of Sea and sky
You are bigger than human understanding.
All things come from you. You can work through all people, even those who don't yet recognise you.
Help the blind to see and the deaf to listen.
Help me to be open to the unexpected. Help me to hear your voice when it comes from unexpected people or places.
Amen

Consider.

Do you believe God works through unbelievers or those with a different belief to you?
How might you respond to a prophetic word given to you by someone who is an unbeliever? Would you recognise it as such?

The effulgent light of Majesty shone into the darkness,
piercing rigidity and rule in its wake.
For those whose eyes were open, radiance was beyond all earthly imagination,
calling them to seek – and follow.

But the blind only saw the jagged darkness, without beauty, only power.
Threat to his Dominion screamed at Herod, slashing at his throat like a blade.
Infant blood leaked from Jerusalem, as a crimson slick,
enveloping the city in a tide of grief.

Purity of the Angels kept Him safe, surrounding him as a cloak,
resting in the warmth of his Fathers palm,
Until the impenetrable blackness slid away,
forging a path of hope, to start at the *new beginning*.

Pam Nicholls

My Prayers – 27th November

NOTES

NOTES

NOTES

Advent Fourteen
28th November

Read or listen to John 1: 1-2, 12-14.
Meditate on the text, dwelling on the words or phrases that stand out to you.

Pray, talk to God about those things that he has brought to you in these verses or use the prayer below if you wish.

Contemplate the text, you may wish to use the suggested consider points to get you started.

Record your exploration of this text using words, prayer, poems, and images.

Prayer.

Lord Jesus
You left the realms of heaven and came to earth as a vulnerable baby. Thank you that through your glory I might become one with you.
As I walk this life path, be with me in every step, helping me to become more like you.
Amen

Consider.

Spend some time thinking about your walk with God.
 How can you take on the divine nature?
 How does being 'at one' with God shape you day by day?

A blank canvas
The ultimate collaboration
Reflecting
Infused
Creating a pulse
An invitation
A welcome
A gift
Acceptance
Belonging
Can you grasp it?
Will you receive it?

Lindsey Morgan-Lundie

My Prayers – 28th November

NOTES

NOTES

NOTES

Advent Fifteen
29ᵗʰ November

Read or listen to John 1: 4 – 5, 9 - 11
Meditate on the text, dwelling on the words or phrases that stand out to you.

Pray, talk to God about those things that he has brought to you in these verses or use the prayer below if you wish.

Contemplate the text, you may wish to use the suggested consider points to get you started.

Record your exploration of this text using words, prayer, poems, and images.

Prayer.

Lord of Light and Hope.
You shine in the depth of all darkness. May I know your light in my life today. Shine into the dark areas of my soul, examine me with gentleness and forgiveness. Help me to accept my shortcomings so that I may live a life that reflects that your light into the darkness of this world. I pray for all those who need your light Lord.
Amen.

Consider.

Spend time thinking about today's verse… what does it mean for this world, so often overshadowed by war, famine, and injustice?

Reflect on what it means to be 'in' the world but not 'of' it.

Morning:
Through the pines, across the Roseland
The palest light shines
Easing aside the darkness -
Gradually, effortlessly -
Until the first spears of light shine through
To embed themselves on the dew-soaked lawn
Glowing the sky with colour
Launching the birds into song.

This is true light,
Just as he is true light
Gradually, effortlessly
Irresistibly
Banishing my darkness
Piercing my heart with truth and love
Glowing me into colour
Launching my life into endless song.

Philip Mountstephen

My Prayers – 29th November

NOTES

NOTES

NOTES

Advent Sixteen
30th November

Read or listen to Luke 17: 20 - 21
Meditate on the text, dwelling on the words or phrases that stand out to you.

Pray, talk to God about those things that he has brought to you in these verses or use the prayer below if you wish.

Contemplate the text, you may wish to use the suggested consider points to get you started.

Record your exploration of this text using words, prayer, poems, and images.

Prayer.

Father in Heaven.
Thy Kingdom come within me,
Thy will be done, within me.
This is my desire, O Lord.
Be with me in my deepest longings.
Make my deepest longing you.
Amen

Consider.

How does the knowledge that Christ's kingdom is within you mean for your life?

How do you recognise Gods will for your life?

Same God in Her Midst

Morning light on Bara.
Flora MacDonald strikes the tinder.
Her fire is lit in the hearth,
She enjoys new warmth in her croft.
Her husband has gone out to fish
And she has many tasks to perform today.
Her day is full,
She is full also.
The flame licks inside her,
She works with joy.
She thinks about Him throughout,
He who is High King of her heart.
All the jobs she will do she does for Him.
The cutting of the wood,
Milking the cows,
Weaving of thick close cloth.
She gives thanks and eats her simple cooked fish.
He tastes so good to her,
And she is satisfied,
She is satisfied.

The central heating clicks on the timer,
Flora MacDonald is up and out with her car keys.
Guitar music synchronises with passing hedgerows.
At work, she inputs information onto a swallowing screen.
Her hands dance with automatic speed and rhythm.
People around her chatter under bright fluorescents.
But she is not listening.
She takes a stroll out into the park,
Finds a bench amid dog walkers and mothers with prams.
She gives thanks, eats, and brushes the crumbs to greedy pigeons.
Her heart is warm inside for her day has been given to Him.
He who is High King of her heart,
And all the jobs she will do she does for Him.
He tastes so good to her.
And she is satisfied,
She is satisfied.

Same God, In her midst, Same God.   *Gillian Barritt*

My Prayers – 30th November

NOTES

NOTES

NOTES

Advent Seventeen
1st December

Read or listen to Romans 8: 8 - 10
Meditate on the text, dwelling on the words or phrases that stand out to you.

Pray, talk to God about those things that he has brought to you in these verses or use the prayer below if you wish.

Contemplate the text, you may wish to use the suggested consider points to get you started.

Record your exploration of this text using words, prayer, poems, and images.

Prayer.

Holy God.
Thank you for choosing me and making me your own.
Help me to be wholly yours. Help me overcome the desires that hinder my life, lead me to live righteously.
Make me holy by the power of your spirit.
Harden my heart to those things which separate me from you.
Fill me lord, with your spirit of truth, hope and love and to live my life according to your holy will.
Amen

Consider.

What "flesh-life' things hamper your journey with God?

Think about the words of confession that you say at church or in private. Do they slip easily off the tongue? Or do they feel inadequate? Do you always feel a burden lifted immediately or does it take time to accept forgiveness?

One in 8 billion

All those people
Too many to imagine
Yet God sees me
Me
Sinful me
I am not so special
Still
Gods spirit is in me
All I had to do was ask
Accept Him in my life
I let Him in
I heard the truth
His spirit will guide
His spirit inside
God in me.
The scales started to tip
Sinful still
But less and less
His spirit helping, guiding
Just me
Becoming more pleasing to God
Not through my own power
But by the Spirit of God
Living in me
Just me
Not special
God in me
The reassurance of knowing
He is on my side
I am being made right with God
Still me
But better
The choice is yours
You too can experience His Spirit
Helping, guiding, comforting
Just ask and accept
Like me.

Debbie MacGregor

My Prayers – 1st December

NOTES

NOTES

NOTES

Advent Eighteen
2nd December

Read or listen to Romans 8: 11
Meditate on the text, dwelling on the words or phrases that stand out to you.

Pray, talk to God about those things that he has brought to you in these verses or use the prayer below if you wish.

Contemplate the text, you may wish to use the suggested consider points to get you started.

Record your exploration of this text using words, prayer, poems, and images.

Prayer.

Risen Lord
Thank you that you gave your life for me.
May the same power that rose you from the dead dwell within me, that I may rise in new life with you.
Fill me with your Holy spirit anew today and banish from me all dark thought.
Amen.

Consider.

Read the verse again, what does it mean to you?
What does it mean to you to know that Christ dwells in you?
How does it affect your daily life?

Waking.

Sleep and darkness cover over
Like a blanket in the cold morning of winter
Muscles reluctant to tense and move
Knowing the cold will seep in and steal
The warm sleep illusion
Of comfort, softness and forever sleep

Then waking comes
Stirring memories of potential
And fulfilment.
Winter is not death, but the bed of new life.

Emerging from the cocoon
Of illusionary warmth,
The cold pierces deep
Drenching bones in the threat of fatigue
Catching breath sharp.

But moments later
In the warmth of that first sip of morning coffee
And the comfort of slippers
Comes the acceptance that this is not the end.

The cold and darkness of this advent is the space
Into which the incarnation is poured.
Into creation.
Into you
and me.

Rev Becca Bell

My Prayers – 2nd December

NOTES

NOTES

NOTES

Advent Nineteen
3rd December

Read or listen to Ephesians 3: 16 - 17
Meditate on the text, dwelling on the words or phrases that stand out to you.

Pray, talk to God about those things that he has brought to you in these verses or use the prayer below if you wish.

Contemplate the text, you may wish to use the suggested consider points to get you started.

Record your exploration of this text using words, prayer, poems, and images.

Prayer.

THREE IN ONE – ONE IN THREE
Thank you that I am grounded and rooted in your love.
Help me to prune those things in my life which prevent me from growing towards your light.
Dwell in my heart Lord, strengthen me by your Holy Spirit, renew me daily with the knowledge of the power of your resurrection. Lead me lord, comfort me, restore me, be in every aspect of my being.
Your love for me knows no bounds.
Let my love for you be unrestrained.
Amen

Consider.

What does it mean to be rooted in Christ and grounded in his love?
How has the knowledge of the resurrection changed you?

The darkness of the night was broken
Your light born to shine
To bring truth, love, and reconciliation
To hearts that yearn to be thine

Hearts that turn towards your face
And open up to receive
Gifts from your glorious riches
Gifts that set us free

Your Spirit dwelling within us
Strengthening our faith from a seed
Shooting roots of love and breaking walls
Healing scars the world cannot see

Preparing our hearts to receive
The presence of your Son
So that we can live a life fulfilled
A life together as one

Caroline Shepherd

My Prayers – 3rd December

NOTES

NOTES

NOTES

Advent Twenty
4th December

Read or listen to Colossians 1: 26 - 27
Meditate on the text, dwelling on the words or phrases that stand out to you.

Pray, talk to God about those things that he has brought to you in these verses or use the prayer below if you wish.

Contemplate the text, you may wish to use the suggested consider points to get you started.

Record your exploration of this text using words, prayer, poems, and images.

Prayer.

God of Mystery
Thank you that you are with me each day.
Help me to be aware of your presence as I go about my day.
You alone are my hope of glory.
Be in my waking, in my sleeping, my thoughts, my words and in my every action.
Amen.

Consider.

What does it mean for God to be in every aspect of our lives?
Do you allow yourself to sense God in every action?

All I see
Inspired by Colossians 1:26-27

Pick, pick at the past picture,
as at the nail that won't get neat,
the scab that won't be smoothed.

Scratch at the old muddy coin,
scraping the familiar face,
once shiny new, now hidden from view.

Unpick the tangled tapestry,
thumbing through the threads,
until appears in part a portrait.

Focus in on those fuzzy scenes,
filter out every nothingy noise,
and finally hear, finally see:

Christ in me, Christ in me,
was then, is now and ever shall be.
Christ in me, the deepest mystery,
the certain hope of future glory.
His face once scuffed and dirty,
his image blurred and faded,
But he's there, he always was,
and now he's all I see,
Christ in me.

Let me pick and unpick
and wipe away the muck
from the self I used to be;
Let me tell the story, not for me
but that he'd be seen
Christ in me.
My hope of glory.

Claire Jones

My Prayers – 4th December

NOTES

NOTES

NOTES

Advent Twenty-One
5th December

Read or listen to 1John 4: 16
Meditate on the text, dwelling on the words or phrases that stand out to you.

Pray, talk to God about those things that he has brought to you in these verses or use the prayer below if you wish.

Contemplate the text, you may wish to use the suggested consider points to get you started.

Record your exploration of this text using words, prayer, poems, and images.

Prayer.

God of Love, Live in me always
God who is Love, show me the way
God of Love, Dwell in me completely
God who is Love, Guide me in your ways
God of Love, compel me to seek you,
All of my days
Amen.

Consider.

'Love one another, as I have loved you'

What do you think Jesus meant when he issued this commandment?
What does love 'look' like in this context?
How easy do you find it to live in love?

WHO can you rely on day by day?
Who **CAN** you rely on week after week?
Who can **YOU** rely on year by year?
God's Word has the answer so let's hear it speak.

The Apostle John wrote his Gospel and several letters too,
He really did know Jesus, through and through.
He wrote in his first letter that **we know and rely** on God's love
Plus, if we live in love we live in God and God will live in US.

Now this is good news for everyone, if we look to God to help us,
He will respond without a doubt; His love could make you really shout.
Not just like frozen peas, soothing a painful area or a satisfying scratching, on an itchy back,
His love is all these things and more, a love that gets you right to the Core.

FOR AS LONG AS WE LET HIM!

Gret Woodason
     06/10/2022

My Prayers – 5th December

NOTES

NOTES

NOTES

Advent Twenty - Two
6th December

Read or listen to John 15: 4 - 5
Meditate on the text, dwelling on the words or phrases that stand out to you.

Pray, talk to God about those things that he has brought to you in these verses or use the prayer below if you wish.

Contemplate the text, you may wish to use the suggested consider points to get you started.

Record your exploration of this text using words, prayer, poems, and images.

Prayer.

Grant to me O Lord your great gifts.
May I love, as you love.
Forgive, with a generous heart
Show restraint, in the face of temptation
Seek Justice, where there is injustice
Act peacefully, where there is discord
Be fruitful in seemingly barren places.
Keep me always seeking Lord.
Amen

Consider.

Is your primary desire to bear fruit for the Lord?
Which parts of your life are bearing no fruit or abundant fruit? Are there areas that need pruning? Or nurturing? Think about how you might achieve this.
When you stand before God…what fruit will you offer him?

Waiting

I am Yours
You are mine
I am the branch
You are the vine.

I wait to feel the power of Your will
So with others Your fruit I may share.
But at times the winds of the world send a chill,
That threatens to leave the branch bare.

Trust and believe, the old song says
So I give You my branch so tender
And I find a peace in patience
A growing strength in surrender.

I don't need to rely on my own strength
For Your life-giving sap will flow
If I do all I do in Your name
Then the fruit of Your love will grow.

Apart from Me you can do nothing, I read,
But we each have our part to play.
For as we need Christ, He needs us too
In showing a lost world His way.

So take our tender branches Lord
Use them to bear Your fruit
Knowing we don't do this work alone
But draw our strength from the root.

For a world that struggles in waiting
A world, at times, so hateful and stressed.
As Christian and Christ grow intertwined
May the world taste Your fruit and know it is blessed.

Jacquie Griffiths

My Prayers – 6th December

NOTES

NOTES

NOTES

Advent Twenty - Three
7th December

Read or listen to John 6: 55 - 57
Meditate on the text, dwelling on the words or phrases that stand out to you.

Pray, talk to God about those things that he has brought to you in these verses or use the prayer below if you wish.

Contemplate the text, you may wish to use the suggested consider points to get you started.

Record your exploration of this text using words, prayer, poems, and images.

Prayer.

Heavenly Father
Thank you that Jesus is the bread of life, and through receiving him we are cleansed from sin and have received everlasting life.
Help me to live my life in such a way that others may too receive this invitation.
All praise and glory belong to you.
Amen.

Consider.

What does it mean to feed on Jesus?

What does the eucharist mean for you?

Invited in

Eat and live
Flesh of my flesh
Bringing energy for fullness of life
Growing you from the inside out
As we become one
Nourishing you on the journey

Drink and live
Blood of my blood
Bringing warmth and love
Resourcing your body and soul
As we become one
Empowering your work in the world

Eat and drink
My Flesh and blood
You in me and I in you
Bringing us ever closer
As we become one
Welcomed home for eternity

Jo Northey

My Prayers – 7th December

NOTES

NOTES

NOTES

Advent Twenty - Four
8th December

Read or listen to 1 John 3. 23 - 24
Meditate on the text, dwelling on the words or phrases that stand out to you.

Pray, talk to God about those things that he has brought to you in these verses or use the prayer below if you wish.

Contemplate the text, you may wish to use the suggested consider points to get you started.

Record your exploration of this text using words, prayer, poems, and images.

Prayer.

Loving God
Thank you that you sent Jesus to pay the price for my sin.
Help me to be obedient to your commands, that your love may flow through me.
Direct me to your will, through the precious gift of your Holy Spirit.
Let me live my life in such a way that you are visible to those around me.
Amen

Consider.

Would others know you are a Christian through your actions alone?
Does your love for others shine through everything that you do?
What stops you from loving some people?

Swimming in December

Plunging deep,
Believing you are there,
To greet me,
To meet me.

Trusting in the depths,
Whispering your name,
Letting the tide take me,
Icy fear then glistening light,
I surrender.
Your love lapping.

Beneath the dark, silent shadows,
The pull of the tide.
Wisdom whispers her safe reasoning,
Take heed:
Ways to avoid the rocks,
Be alert.
Watch out for the floundering.

Abide and bask in safe waters.
Rest and float,
Stretch out into the glistening silvered silk,
Watch and wonder in the hidden underwater places.
Immersed.
Receive in awe.

Only to return to the shore, once more,
A salty secret to share.
Life flowing,
Bursting forth,
Chattering, shivering, grinning.
Alive.

Jo Thomas. A wild sea swimmer

My Prayers – 8th December

NOTES

NOTES

NOTES

Advent Twenty - Five
9th December

Read or listen to 1 John 4: 14 - 15
Meditate on the text, dwelling on the words or phrases that stand out to you.

Pray, talk to God about those things that he has brought to you in these verses or use the prayer below if you wish.

Contemplate the text, you may wish to use the suggested consider points to get you started.

Record your exploration of this text using words, prayer, poems, and images.

Prayer.

Heavenly Father
I offer up praise and thanks that Christ came to earth to live and die in my place.
Thank you that you paid the price for all sin.
Quench my spiritual thirst and fill me with your water. Renew a right spirit within me and keep me in life eternal.
Amen

Consider.

How often do you say the creed? When did you last really consider the words?
Try saying it now, listen to the words you are saying. What do you find easy to believe? Which lines challenge you most?

Home

Hearth light, darkening sky
Drizzle wet, curlew cry
Winter grey, rug warm
Holy hope, Advent home

Heart home, can you see?
Saving grace, David's key
Love intwined, heaven here
Open mouthed, God come near

Son of God, human face
Open heart, make space
Door knock, I can see
Jesus Christ, abide in me

Hugh Nelson

My Prayers – 9th December

NOTES

NOTES

NOTES

Advent Twenty - Six
10^h December

Read or listen to Luke 12: 39 - 40
Meditate on the text, dwelling on the words or phrases that stand out to you.

Pray, talk to God about those things that he has brought to you in these verses or use the prayer below if you wish.

Contemplate the text, you may wish to use the suggested consider points to get you started.

Record your exploration of this text using words, prayer, poems, and images.

Prayer.

Eternal God
With grateful heart, I thank you for the many blessings I have received. I pray for the grace to be aware of the responsibility they bring. Bless my work Lord.
Grant that I may live in such a way that when it comes to the end of my time here on earth, I may not be fearful of your coming, but full of joy.
Amen

Consider.

Jesus will return at the end of time but hasn't left us either.
How does this influence how you live your life? Are you prepared for the end time? Do you keep watch?
Do you find this reading uncomfortable? Why?

Jesus taught with story and parable
Of how us humans can be so fallible
And disciple Luke retold told the story
Of when the Lord will return in glory

Beware the thief in the master's home
When he arrived, well that's not known
He should have been barred from within
The servants weren't prepared for him

Now if we knew his arrival day
We'd get things done and squared away
But knoweth not when the day will come
When again we'll see God's only son

We must be alert and be prepared
For the one our faith declared
His coming in which we believe
Our lives wide open to receive

When we open up our hearts to him
No panic rush, all's fine and trim
Then what joy we shall attain
When Jesus is with us again

David Remick

My Prayers – 10th December

NOTES

NOTES

NOTES

Advent Twenty - Seven
11th December

Read or listen to Matthew 25: 1 - 13
Meditate on the text, dwelling on the words or phrases that stand out to you.

Pray, talk to God about those things that he has brought to you in these verses or use the prayer below if you wish.

Contemplate the text, you may wish to use the suggested consider points to get you started.

Record your exploration of this text using words, prayer, poems, and images.

Prayer.

Lord,
Give me the grace today to look for you in every encounter.
Help me to be more diligent in prayer and grant me patience as I await your response.
I thank you for all those I rely on day by day, and give you thanks that they are in my life.
Keep me alert lord.
Amen.

Consider.

Why are the five bridesmaids considered foolish?

What is the oil in your lamp?
 Is it prayer? Time? Or something else?

Waiting.
Constantly waiting,
filling candles with oil.
Praying. Waiting.
Be on your guard, they say
Stay alert, they proclaim.
Waiting in the darkness.
Anxiously waiting.

The way is narrow.
Dark.
Rocky it be and uneven.
Stumbling, falling in darkness:
Waiting for someone to bring light.

Not prepared for this amount of darkness.
Lack of expectation.
Lack of preparation.

Struggling.
Now seeing the lights of others.
A distant memory stirs.
Small lights moving to the great Light.
Demon of darkness disappear.

Awake and alert for the first time,
even with a heavy burden,
Moving with confidence and joy:
towards the Light source.
The Light that shines in the darkness
And the darkness has not overcome in.

Brian Davis Penlee cluster : Penzance

T   Too late to prepare ,
O   out come
O   Overcome

L   Look, Learn, listen, love
A   Anxious, Anxiety, , Apathetic
T   Turn again, truth to power
E   Extinction Rebellion, Exit,

Penlee cluster group poem

My Prayers – 11th December

NOTES

NOTES

Advent Twenty - Eight
12ʰ December

Read or listen to Luke 21:25
Meditate on the text, dwelling on the words or phrases that stand out to you.

Pray, talk to God about those things that he has brought to you in these verses or use the prayer below if you wish.

Contemplate the text, you may wish to use the suggested consider points to get you started.

Record your exploration of this text using words, prayer, poems, and images.

Prayer.

Maker of Heaven and Earth.
Help me to see you in the world around me. Help me to ground myself in your love and give me the ability to listen for your encouragements and in your warnings.
As Advent advances and I focus on preparing to celebrate your birth on earth, help me to remember to also be prepared for that glorious day when you will come again.
Amen

Consider.

How do you need Jesus to come into your life this Christmas?
Do you look for signs and wonders?
What words do you long to hear when Jesus comes for you?

We all look for signs to appear
in the sun, moon, and skies
We often miss the one we need most
shining right before our eyes
We live in fear of the unknown
Fear that spreads between man
So, love we forget to show,
and darkness fills our lands
Amongst the pain and suffering
of those who peril in this sea
There is always a light of chance and change,
a good to set us free.
When we come together as one
 who share in Skies and seas
We can raise each other up
 and our saviour we may see
No more at war within our hearts
or on each other's lands
We join together in one song
 child woman and man.
When that day does come to pass
in every tribe and tongue
We come together to worship him
 and his praises will be sung
No more the fear of the unknown
Of the skies, sea, or land
We join together in peace and love
 to be received by God's unwavering hand.

Ellouise Allard

My Prayers – 12th December

NOTES

NOTES

NOTES

Advent Twenty - Nine
13th December

Read or listen to 1 Thessalonians 4: 14 - 16
Meditate on the text, dwelling on the words or phrases that stand out to you.

Pray, talk to God about those things that he has brought to you in these verses or use the prayer below if you wish.

Contemplate the text, you may wish to use the suggested consider points to get you started.

Record your exploration of this text using words, prayer, poems, and images.

Prayer.

Loving Father
I thank you that death has no sting for those who will be raised by the same almighty power that raised Christ from the dead.
Protect my body, mind, and spirit today and always, draw me closer to you as I walk this path.
Amen

Consider.

It is not always easy to think about death, especially our own. Gently think about the time when you will be resurrected, how do you imagine it? Does it occur in a physical place that you love? Think about those spaces where you find God easily, thin places where heaven and earth meet.

Waiting now, to celebrate the birth of Jesus,
God made flesh to dwell amongst our humanity.
Waiting now, for lights, music, and celebration,
Filled with the hope and expectation of this season.
Waiting now, for my God who knows me,
Who sees my life and gets involved when I invite Him.
Each year I wait, and then I celebrate.

Yet what is this sound of trumpets?
Angels' song, hosanna cries, a splitting of the skies?

Waiting now, for the loud command,
Jesus my returning King.
Waiting now, for His sleeping ones to rise,
To enter His glory, of which they sing.
Waiting now for my name to be called,
To be swept up in a great cloud.
Trumpets blaring, Choirs of Angels singing,
Oh, what a great and glorious Final day!
No more waiting, the day of Jubilee has come.

A St Martin's Church Life Group, Liskeard.

My Prayers – 13th December

NOTES

NOTES

NOTES

Advent Thirty
14th December

Read or listen to James 5: 7 - 8
Meditate on the text, dwelling on the words or phrases that stand out to you.

Pray, talk to God about those things that he has brought to you in these verses or use the prayer below if you wish.

Contemplate the text, you may wish to use the suggested consider points to get you started.

Record your exploration of this text using words, prayer, poems, and images.

Prayer.

Breath of love and hope.
Thank you for your patience with me when I am slow to catch on to your will for me.
I pray that I may be blessed with patience and the endurance I need to walk closer with you to perfect my faith.
Help me to be more like the farmer who patiently waits, and help me to trust you in all matters, that you may bring forth fruit in me.
Amen.

Consider.

How patient are you? Is patience something you find easy? Or is it something you really struggle with?
Spend a few moments thinking about times you have been impatient with your waiting. Would being patient have changed the outcome or drawn you closer to God?

Patience in Suffering by Karen Austin

If you haven't experienced suffering,
you haven't experienced blessing.
For where there is a rainbow,
there has been rain.

It is never very easy.
It is rarely invited.
But where there is power,
There has usually been pain.

He knows that we are aching,
And he cries a silent tear.
But He has trod the path before us,
we really need not fear.

For His love is all around us,
Through the day and through the night.
He simply stills and calms us.
He will give us strength and might.

The mountain may be very steep.
The path seems lost from view.
But He encourages us to pause,
prepare for something new.

For, over the crest of that steep climb.
is a flat and easier way.
Dig in, dig deep, keep going.
To Him your fears allay.

Precious child of God ... remember...
He will give you Angels by your side.
You are unconditionally loved,
And He will never ever forsake you.
Take Courage,
Have Patience,
He will be your Guide.

My Prayers – 14th December

NOTES

NOTES

NOTES

Advent Thirty - One
15th December

Read or listen to 2 Peter 3: 10 - 13
Meditate on the text, dwelling on the words or phrases that stand out to you.

Pray, talk to God about those things that he has brought to you in these verses or use the prayer below if you wish.

Contemplate the text, you may wish to use the suggested consider points to get you started.

Record your exploration of this text using words, prayer, poems, and images.

Prayer.

Heavenly Father
Thank you for your word, laying out your perfect plan for the world.
Thank you for the gifts of redemption and salvation.
Help me to remember that one day all the trials and troubles of the world will cease, but in the meantime help me to live my life in a way that points to you.
May I honour your holy name in all that I do, say and think.
Amen.

Consider.

Spend some time in quiet contemplation, ask the Holy Spirit to reveal the areas in your life where you are living a holy and godly life and those areas where you could grow in faithfulness.

Advent is a time of waiting
Of hope, of excitement;
Our King coming as a baby
First heard be lowly Shepherds – not knowing what it meant.

They ran to see the King
They worshipped and adored;
They didn't know this was to be
The one who came to save – their saviour and their Lord.

Sometimes we live, regardless
Of what the future holds;
May we head your warning
Of living Holy lives – as our future lives unfolds.

Each day is not a given
Each day is lent by You
For us to be the people
We are put on earth to be – Messengers pure and true.

As we look forward to the Babe
With hopeful, eager hearts;
May we look forward also
To a new heaven and earth – that loving You imparts

Pastor Jenny

My Prayers – 15ᵗʰ December

NOTES

NOTES

NOTES

Advent Thirty - Two
16th December

Read or listen to Revelation 22: 11 - 13
Meditate on the text, dwelling on the words or phrases that stand out to you.

Pray, talk to God about those things that he has brought to you in these verses or use the prayer below if you wish.

Contemplate the text, you may wish to use the suggested consider points to get you started.

Record your exploration of this text using words, prayer, poems, and images.

Prayer.

My Lord and my God. I marvel in wonder that you left your heavenly throne to suffer a life of humiliation and death. Help me to live as you did, sowing seeds of faith and guiding your people. Thank you for dying for my sin and for your gift of eternal life. Help me to live in your ways and to imitate your life as I await your return.
Amen

Consider.

"Alpha and Omega", "First and Last", "Beginning and End"
How do these descriptions of the Almighty make you feel?
Have you got a favoured way of describing God?
What other names for God can you think of? Write them down, see how many of the 950 names for God you know. (Then check on google for the ones you don't know)

Waiting.

Waiting.
In the silence of the night, thoughts thunder.
Deafening, but only to the one from which they come.
Without distraction from the daily noise,
They echo and grow.
Could I have, Should I have, have I been?
Answers are not forthcoming from the one who posed the question.
Be still and know that you are loved.
The morning will come, along with the answers,
But the wait feels like forever.
The certainty of daybreak, the beginning, and the end,
But not yet.
Hour, after hour, after hour,
Waiting for the light to shine and the darkness to pass
I am coming soon.
The Child and the children, rejoice together,
As the night has passed.
The reward, the gift, given to all,
Love.
The fears, the worries, uncertainties, doubt.
Gone in the fraction of a second,
in the presence of God.
Amen.

Rev. Robin Thwaites

My Prayers – 16th December

NOTES

NOTES

NOTES

Advent Thirty - Three
17th December

Read or listen to Daniel 12: 1 - 3
Meditate on the text, dwelling on the words or phrases that stand out to you.

Pray, talk to God about those things that he has brought to you in these verses or use the prayer below if you wish.

Contemplate the text, you may wish to use the suggested consider points to get you started.

Record your exploration of this text using words, prayer, poems, and images.

Prayer.

Lord of Light and Love
Thank you for the words in Daniel. Thank you that you offer me such protection. Help me to stay awake to the signs of your kingdom. Help me to walk in your light, that you may be seen in me by all those I encounter. May my actions reflect your kingdom. Help me to invite people to your table Lord.
Be with all those who are seeking you this day.
Amen.

Consider.

What do you believe about angels? What is their role?
How would you expect one to look?
Do you ever ask for angels to protect you?

Response to Daniel 12: 1-3
on the Eve of St Michael and All Angels

Interrupted tossed filled night.
Broken fitful sleep:
product of late-night media.
Eye catching bold headlines:
economic crisis, wars, natural disasters.
inhumanity upon inhumanity.
Alarming responses tumble out:
voices and "likes" of blue light night,
self-obsessed social media wade in.
Captivating, drug-like.
Doomed earth, doomed humanity.
Pontificating in godlike strength
always the fault of someone else.

From nowhere and unplanned blue tech screen fades.
Battery dies giving rise to total darkness.
Entering instead into mystery and silence of the night.
Time to sit with them weight of world issues.
Alone.

Starlight from pollution free skies fill this space.
Noticed for the first time.
Captivating, spell binding.
Stilling. Stilling.
Logical trained night knowledge crashes through the brain
naming each constellation.
Vain attempt to control the natural order
and escape this God tingled moment.

This Eve of St Michael and All Angels,
bible text subliminal in brain.
Angels come in many guises.
Peace. Peace be with you.
Rest with me under this star filled galaxy
I, whose name is Love,
Written on every star beam,

To a hungry broken war-torn world.
From the beginning of time.
I Am:
embracing each person, each crisis.
as a parent holds a precious newborn.
The sounds of night doom give way
to encompassing warm filled silence.
Perfumed fragrance fills the air:
enduring life enhancing angel's message of peace.

I Am
your God.
All will be well,
all manner of things shall be well.

Sian Yates

My Prayers – 17th December

NOTES

NOTES

NOTES

NOTES

Advent Thirty - Four
18th December

Read or listen to Philippians 1: 9 - 11
Meditate on the text, dwelling on the words or phrases that stand out to you.

Pray, talk to God about those things that he has brought to you in these verses or use the prayer below if you wish.

Contemplate the text, you may wish to use the suggested consider points to get you started.

Record your exploration of this text using words, prayer, poems, and images.

Prayer.

Heavenly Father
I thank you for that I can come before you in prayer and deepen my relationship with you.
Help me to grow in knowledge and understanding so that I may support others in their journey with you. Thank you for all those who have pointed me toward you in my journey so far. Use me Lord, in all ways, that I may produce fruitful relationships.
Amen.

Consider.

Do you have someone who journeys with you? A spiritual director, another Christian? How often do you spend time with them?
Spend a few moments now praying for them and thanking God for the ways that guidance shapes you.
If you do not have this sort of person in your life, think about who has inspired you on your Christian journey and give thanks for them.

harvest of righteousness

Carved rock,
slate, and glass is not
the planting of the Lord, yet
these hallowed hollowed gothic barns
are the Jabbock of our struggle, our nuptial Cana,
they sign the landscape of life, of faith, the Bethany of our loss.
Seeds planted prayerfully by those who knew
they would not see the crop,
and now do not see
how few, how
cropped,
we are.

Granite,
dug into soil,
yields little.

Love,
poured out,
unfolds hope.

Simon Cade

My Prayers – 18th December

NOTES

NOTES

NOTES

Advent Thirty - Five
19th December

Read or listen to 1 Corinthians 1: 6 - 8
Meditate on the text, dwelling on the words or phrases that stand out to you.

Pray, talk to God about those things that he has brought to you in these verses or use the prayer below if you wish.

Contemplate the text, you may wish to use the suggested consider points to get you started.

Record your exploration of this text using words, prayer, poems, and images.

Prayer.

Search me, O Lord, and show me those aspects of my life which do not glorify you. Thank you for the continuity of your promise to me, however many times I fall.
During the dark nights that lay before me, and the summer nights that are to come, you have promised to keep and sustain me.
As we get closer to celebrating your birth, fill my heart with joy and wonder again.
Amen.

Consider.

It is easy to get caught up in the busyness of Christmas. Cold, damp days, crisp dark nights. Shops full of noise and the glare of harsh lights. STOP! Think through your memories to a time when none of the responsibilities of the celebrations belonged to you. Can you remember the thrill of anticipation and wonder as you eagerly awaited Jesus' birth? How can you bring hope, wonder and expectation to others and to yourself this year?

Buffering

I listen and discern, trying to cut through the wheat and the Chaff, wielding my scythe.
The scythe distracts my path and gifts, shining and sharp, glistening in the sun
I admire its power and strength its ability…. Buffering

It arrives whirling, whirring, questioning, jumping up and down like a toddler in a tantrum, bullish racing thoughts rampaging like a self-obsessed bulldozer.
Breathe, focus, embrace the difference, the neuro diversity, surrender, I am his perfectly made.

I Give thanks to my precious lord, the spirit comes, sublime spiritual buzzing sensations behind my ear.
You are unafraid, a roaring lion full to fight, to defend, but as gentle as a summer breeze, nurturing like a mother to its child, Find the lost, Love and keep it simple.

Yes, use me as your vessel Lord I am yours. Buffering but yours.
The spirit flows, soft words come, whispers of wait, be patient. Perfectly Imperfect, "work in progress"
The signal is steadfast, the buffering is inclusive. I am his child and wait for him to come.

NB: How to stop buffering
1.turn it off and turn it back on
2.make sure no applications are running in the background
3.Disconnect other devices from the network
3.delete your cache and temporary files
4.Reduce Video quality
5.Download content instead of streaming

Joanna Swan

My Prayers – 19th December

NOTES

NOTES

NOTES

Advent Thirty - Six
20th December

Read or listen to John 10: 22 - 30
Meditate on the text, dwelling on the words or phrases that stand out to you.

Pray, talk to God about those things that he has brought to you in these verses or use the prayer below if you wish.

Contemplate the text, you may wish to use the suggested consider points to get you started.

Record your exploration of this text using words, prayer, poems, and images.

Prayer.

Lord, thank you that through the gift of faith you reveal yourself to me. Help me to trust that you will respond to my prayers, giving me patience and persistence in my praying. Help me to accept there isn't always an easy answer to the difficulties I face. Help me to hear your voice when you call.
Be with me Lord, in my doubt and in my belief.
Amen

Consider.

How well do you listen for God? Do you have a place that you regularly use for prayer? By having a special place to pray can train your body to pray. When you enter your prayer space your body receives the signal that it is time to pray. This can have a significant impact on you as there will be times in your life when praying does not come easily. Think about your holy place.

Where are **your** temple courts today? Where is **your** holy place?
What have you put within them, or are they just an empty space?
Have you built high walls around them, where nothing can reside?
No light, no sound, no comfort. No memorial deep inside?

But candles are lit in winter: whilst remembering in the dark;
illuminating your sacred place; a dedication in your heart.
Honouring what has gone before, yet treasuring the present;
remembering the 'Miracle' with emotion, incandescent.

Some were waiting and some were looking; sometimes searching, but couldn't see
that before them stood their God; their King, for all eternity.
I thank him that he is my Shepherd; am grateful now I'm his sheep;
am safe now in the knowledge, that my eternal soul he'll keep.

This Advent marks his coming; being born in a body of 'flesh':
a candle lit in our darkness midst that humble, but sacred place.
Tell us you're the Messiah? The stars shout out your name!
But still, some waited in suspense, in case their Saviour came!

So, honour what has gone before; but treasure too, the present.
Remember always that Miracle - his birth bringing luminescence.
This Advent brings no candle flame, flickering with doubt
but a sure and constant memory that nothing can put out.

This is Jesus: Light of **our** world; Our Saviour; God's own Son.
Our Servant Queen recognised him and everything he'd done.
She knew his voice and followed him; served him first, before all other.
Will you listen still to her deep faith, this nation's spiritual Mother?

Maggie Dolbear. 5th October 2022.

My Prayers – 20th December

NOTES

NOTES

NOTES

Advent Thirty - Seven
21st December

Read or listen to John 1: 5, 9 and John 16:33
Meditate on the text, dwelling on the words or phrases that stand out to you.

Pray, talk to God about those things that he has brought to you in these verses or use the prayer below if you wish.

Contemplate the text, you may wish to use the suggested consider points to get you started.

Record your exploration of this text using words, prayer, poems, and images.

Prayer.

God of light and love.
Thank you for the gift of light, given to me in Jesus.
Thank you for all the gifts I have received this past year. Thank you for guiding me through the difficult times. I ask that you continue to light my path as I walk with you and fill me with the desire to shine your light into the darkness of the people and places around me.
I live in hope of the coming light.
Amen.

Consider.

Darkness is simply the lack of light.
We all have hidden areas in our lives where darkness overcomes us. Spend some time asking Jesus to illuminate these areas and invite him to be the perpetual light in your life.
How can you be a light of hope in the darkness for others in these difficult times?

Radiant Mother

She groans
To stand in the half light,
Searching.

She bears
The lamp, light
Flickering.

The light splutters, gutters,
Slowly, excruciatingly
Dying
To darkness,
Pieta.

She cradles
Her swollen belly, feet inside
Moving.

She sees
The new light
Radiating forgiveness

To all –
Perfect peace.

Margaret Miles

My Prayers – 21st December

NOTES

NOTES

NOTES

Advent Thirty - Eight
22nd December

Read or listen to Luke 1: 26 - 49
Meditate on the text, dwelling on the words or phrases that stand out to you.

Pray, talk to God about those things that he has brought to you in these verses or use the prayer below if you wish.

Contemplate the text, you may wish to use the suggested consider points to get you started.

Record your exploration of this text using words, prayer, poems, and images.

Prayer.

Loving God, Heavenly Mother,
Thank you that your love is fierce, strong and offers me protection and hope. Help me answer your continued call on my life with the conviction that Mary showed when she agreed to do your will. Give me a quiet resilience as I face the business of the coming festivities. Help me to rest so that I may face each day with the renewed energy to say, "Here I am, servant of the Lord".
Amen

Consider.

Thank God for the women who have loved, supported, and guided you through your faith journey.

Are you ready to say anew, "Here I am. Servant of the Lord"?

Mary's "Yes"

I wonder how it would feel,
to say 'Yes', like Mary did?
To not be concerned
with the 'what', 'when' 'where' or 'why'?
No detail required;
just complete acceptance
of the answered 'how?'.

I wonder how it would feel,
to say 'Yes', like Mary did?
To not be concerned
with what others thought and spoke
about my situation?
Knowing it made no difference
to your love for me.

I wonder how it would feel,
to say 'Yes', like Mary did?
To not be concerned
with the waiting or the journey,
or the task you set before me?
Knowing that I could trust you
not to break your word.

I wonder how it would feel,
to say 'Yes', like Mary did?
To not be concerned
with whom, what, I was leaving
behind as I walked your way?
Knowing you were beside me
with each taken step.

I wonder how it would feel,
to reach the destination?
To have understood
this was always where it led?
No detail required.
just complete acceptance
for what will come next.

I wonder how it would feel
To have Mary's simple trust
in the God I know
knew me before I was born?
To believe that I am loved,
to believe that I am worthy -
every single day?

I wonder how it would feel,
If I wasn't too scared
of human rejection?
If I realised, I was good enough?
If I understood
the dreams and plans you have for me?
If I simply followed you?

I wonder how it would feel
If I said 'Yes'?

Kay Short

My Prayers – 22nd December

NOTES

NOTES

NOTES

NOTES

Advent Thirty - Nine
23rd December

Read or listen to 1 Corinthians 12: 1 - 11
Meditate on the text, dwelling on the words or phrases that stand out to you.

Pray, talk to God about those things that he has brought to you in these verses or use the prayer below if you wish.

Contemplate the text, you may wish to use the suggested consider points to get you started.

Record your exploration of this text using words, prayer, poems, and images.

Prayer.

Gracious and Generous God.
I thank you for all the gifts that you have bestowed on me. I thank you too for all the gifts that I have been given by others. Let me be reminded in this season of giving that the gift of your birth in the world is there for me to receive each day. Help me to have a more generous heart Lord, help me to give to others joyfully and fully. Amen.

Consider.

I am sure you are super organised, and all your gifts are wrapped by now. Are you someone who puts real thought into a gift, or do you do a last-minute dash buying up whatever is left on the shelves? Do you take more care over some gifts than others?
As you give your gifts this season, take time to focus and ponder on the spiritual gifts you have been given.

As I clear the last traces
Of paper from the gifts unwrapped
I take a moment to peel back the layers
Of the gifts divinely bestowed on me.

Thank you, Lord, for wisdom
For without it no doubt
There would have been an injury
When baby threw a sprout.

Thank you, Lord, for miracles
I really needed one
When I realised that the turkey
Was totally underdone!

Thank you for the gift of tongues
It really wasn't the booze
That jumbled up my words
As I led the thanks for food.

Thank you for the gift of patience
As the final Lego piece is placed
I walk in stockinged feet away
Treading on the tiny brick, mislaid

Before I fall exhausted
And sleep for time infinity
One more gift I ask for Lord
To understand the Trinity

Thank you for these gifts and more
That you have given me
Help me to use them Lord
To set your people free

Claire Burgess

My Prayers – 23rd December

NOTES

NOTES

NOTES

Advent Forty
24th December

Read or listen to Isaiah 9; 6 - 7
Meditate on the text, dwelling on the words or phrases that stand out to you.

Pray, talk to God about those things that he has brought to you in these verses or use the prayer below if you wish.

Contemplate the text, you may wish to use the suggested consider points to get you started.

Record your exploration of this text using words, prayer, poems, and images.

Prayer.

Holy God on this most holy of nights,
Help me to be once again renewed by the wonder of your humble birth. Thank you that you stepped into our world to uphold justice and righteousness. Guide me as I continue to follow you.
May I rest this night, knowing the joy that I shall feel in the morning when I hear those word. "Unto us a child is born"
Amen.

Consider.

As we reach the end of this Advent journey, look back at the notes you have taken, the prayers or poems you have written, or the pictures you have drawn.
Spend some quiet time with God, rest peacefully, so that you are ready to welcome the Christ child in the morning.

"For unto us a child is born."

Millenia past, yet still so true,
The words the prophet spoke to few
Who held the message, tried to live
As he had told that God would give
To each and every soul on earth
A chance for peace, for life, for birth:
Birth into realms of endless peace
Where justice rules with love's increase;
For God's own son to us is given,
A light to show that what was hidden
Is man's own selfish, inward view;
But in that light we must renew
Our view on what our God has done,
And does so freely, through his Son;
Who, born among us, loves us all;
The black, the white, the faithless; all
Can truly bring, through Advent prayer,
A world where not one soul despair.

Martyn Pinnock

My Prayers – 24th December

NOTES

NOTES

NOTES

Wishing you and those you hold dear, a Blessed Christmas